The following practice exam features 45 sample questions to help in preparation for taking the CIPP/US certification exam. These questions are not taken directly from the test and you should not expect to see these questions on the exam. They merely reflect the subject matter and style/format of the questions that you might expect to see on the exam. This practice exam is in no way affiliated with the International Association of Privacy Professionals (IAPP). Your scores on this practice exam are in no way predictive of how you will perform on the actual CIPP/US exam.

The questions have been broken out by domain to roughly proportionally represent the way they will be apportioned on the exam. All of the answers will be explained at the end of the practice exam, along with some helpful tips and guidance.

Before answering the following exam questions pay attention to qualifiers such as **best, most, least, most likely, least likely, except**, etc.

1) A newly hired Privacy Manager for a private commercial company doing business across the US has been tasked with continuously updating the company's privacy policies based on the latest laws and regulations. To accomplish this, the privacy manager should pay closest attention to:

    A) Local city council initiatives
    B) Proposed legislation being debated in the US House of Representatives
    C) A tort case being litigated in the US Supreme Court
    D) A proposed tax law the state's governor has threatened to veto

2) A company based in Minneapolis, MN is facing FTC enforcement action after numerous consumer complaints. The company is most likely facing these actions because:

A) Consumers received direct advertisements from an affiliated company after agreeing online they had the option, and then declining to opt in to receive such advertisements
B) Consumers had billing disputes that the customer service department was not able to resolve
C) Consumers have lodged repeated complaints about the accessibility of the company's mobile version of the website
D) The company's CEO insulted the FTC chairman on social media

3) The New Mexico legislature passes a new wide-ranging privacy law the governor has
signed. As a privacy professional working in the state, it is most important to understand:

A) What the final vote count was
B) What other companies in your industry are doing to be compliant with the new
law
C) The specific types of information covered by the law and who enforces potential
violations
D) Whether the full text of the law is available online in PDF format or whether you
should order a paper copy

4) A litigant has their case dismissed after the judge cites a dozen similar cases that were found
to be dismissed for lack of standing. This can be best described as an example of

A) Case Law
B) Statutory Law
C) Arbitration Law
D) Common Law

5) Mr. Smith is in a longstanding dispute with his neighbor Mr. Jones, about the location of the fenceline separating their respective properties. Mr. Jones has insisted for years that the actual position of the fenceline should be 20 ft. further away than the fence is currently positioned. One day Mr. Smith is served with paperwork summoning him to court over the matter. Mr. Smith could ultimately face:

    A) 30 days in jail for illegal placement of the fence
    B) A judgement ordering him to move the fence at his own expense or an equivalent amount owed to Mr. Jones to accomplish this
    C) A lengthy arbitration battle over where the fence should be located
    D) A court decision forfeiting his house and land to be auctioned by the county

6) ACME Widgets Incorporated had lax security protocols until Jane was finally promoted to VP of Privacy. Jane is hard at work overhauling the company's security protocols, but in the meantime the federal government has informed the company it is culpable for negligence of their previously existing policies citing numerous violations. The CEO has asked Jane to resolve this issue as quickly and expeditiously as possible, while minimizing bad press. In order to accomplish this task, the best course of action would be:

A) Hiring the best corporate defense lawyers and taking the case to court
B) Agreeing to stop the negligent actions and pay a fine, without officially admitting wrongdoing
C) Promising to stop the negligent actions which will likely lead the government to lose interest and move on to other more important matters
D) Initiate a highly visible media campaign to tout ACME's new and improved privacy standards you've implemented, which should convince the government to drop the case

7) You have just been hired as a privacy professional for a company that has recently merged
   with another company, assuming control of massive amounts of data. In order to organize
   and get a handle on the data, you should implement a plan to:

   A) Call the data security officers at the old company that you merged with and see
      what their data management plans were
   B) Shop for the best data organization software on the market
   C) Do a full inventory of all the data in your possession and organize it according to
      sensitivity, figure out the flows of data within your organization, and create an
      accountability plan for safeguarding it
   D) Do an inventory only of the data you deem relevant, using your professional
      judgement, so as not to waste time and company resources

8) What is the best reason to encrypt sensitive data?

A) Protection from liability after a breach according to many state laws
B) Insurance in case a disgruntled employee leaves with a trove of proprietary data
C) Encryption is a fast-rising buzzword in the privacy world, and companies that use it are seen more favorably
D) Encryption is only useful in rare, specific circumstances and should not be a major priority in developing a privacy plan

9) The best way to communicate the specifics of your company's privacy plan to consumers and
stakeholders is:

    A) Contact every individual directly and explain the privacy plan in detail, allowing
       for questions and comments during a specified time period
    B) Create a Privacy Notice that individuals can access upon request
    C) Create a Privacy Notice to be displayed on the company website and posted
       physically in areas where customers and employees can see it
    D) Communication of the specifics of your company's privacy plan is unnecessary,
       it's sufficient to merely have one

10) Which of the following is not an example of when a consumer must be given the opportunity
to "opt in" to sharing personal information?

A) When a website is collecting info on children under 13
B) Before an individual receives marketing emails on a regular basis
C) When a health insurance company shares a customer's health information with a
medical device company relevant to the customer's healthcare needs
D) All of the above are examples when individuals must be asked to "opt-in" to
sharing their personal information

11) When a prospective employer runs a background check as part of their screening process, that employer is legally obligated to do all of the following except:

    A) Receive express written permission to conduct the background check before doing so

    B) Inform the candidate if they did not get an offer of employment based on results of the background check

    C) Inform the individual of ways they could improve their credit regardless of their credit score or results of the background check

    D) All of the above are legal obligations of prospective employers

12) The best source of rules and statutes for consumers to have access to the information entities have collected on them and to challenge or correct that information are:

A) Overarching federal or multi-national laws that govern the rights of access and redress
B) Fair Information Practice organizations that develop specific guidelines or principles that address consumer access and redress
C) Corporate bylaws that prioritize consumer rights
D) Altruistic privacy professionals who go above and beyond to incorporate these policies, written or unwritten, regardless of corporate mandate or law

13) What are the most likely methods of ensuring an outside vendor will uphold privacy laws
and standards to minimize the risk of beaches?

    A) Do background research on the vendor and have them sign a contract with the
same privacy standard language as exists within the company's primary privacy
policies
    B) Cultivate personal relationships with the vendor's upper management members
and get their personal assurances they will take privacy as seriously as you do
    C) Have regular meetings/lunches with the vendor to discuss privacy issues and
safeguards
    D) Trust the vendor and do not micromanage them. Their reputation is at stake so
you can rest assured they will take privacy seriously

Please answer the following 3 questions based on the following scenario:

Jake was starting up his first telemarketing sales firm and was eager to get things up and running. He procured some office space, bought 20 computers, got the VoIP telephone system installed, all the proper licensing, and went about finding a VP to run day-to-day operations. He enlisted the help of his college buddy and fellow business major, Vishal. Vishal was concerned about the rapid pace at which Jake was pushing full steam ahead in setting up the business. He was also concerned that Jake had not thoroughly read and absorbed all the Maryland state laws that would apply to their business venture.

Jake urged Vishal not to worry, and pushed him to expedite the process of training and hiring staff. Vishal, with reservations, began the process. On a very tight timeline, Vishal made the best decisions he could under the circumstances and hired 20 telemarketers. He could not find a sufficient candidate for a floor manager, so he decided to take on the role himself. Although the process was rushed, Vishal found a reputable firm he was able to confirm was a licensed CRA to conduct the background checks and everyone he hired was cleared before being offered employment. Next Vishal set out to create a robust training program that emphasized internet and computer security. After all, every computer would be housing proprietary company information as well as sensitive customer information.

Jake resisted, telling Vishal "We need to get them on the phones. These are smart people. They're tech savvy. You hired them, and I trust you!" Vihsal grew more concerned, but relented. He decided to forgo the official security training he had designed and just posted security tips around the sales floor and sent out company-wide emails, occasionally reminding staff individually in passing to take IT security seriously. For all intents and purposes, he was the IT and IT Security department, in addition to being the de facto HR department and floor manager. Vishal crossed his fingers and hoped for the best. Before long, some problems emerged. Vishal noticed the same login credentials being used on multiple computers. One employee no call/no showed and had a removable hard drive containing private customer information with them. Several employees had found ways to get around the internet filter and access sites that were not at all business related for excessive periods of time. Vishal confronted Jake with this info but he seemed mostly unconcerned. "Sales are good! I'm sure you can handle this stuff."

Then one day Vishal came to work and logged into his computer and saw an ominous message on the screen: "YOUR ESSENTIAL FILES HAVE BEEN ENCRYPTED. IN ORDER TO RECOVER YOUR FILES YOU MUST DEPOSIT $5,000 WORTH OF BITCOIN TO THE FOLLOWING ACCOUNT #." He was unable to access any business-related files or programs. Vishal walked out onto the sales floor to discover all his employees locked out of their systems with the same message as his displayed on their monitors. Vishal went to Jake's office and knocked on the door. "We have a problem," he said.

14) What is the most likely cause of the ransomware attack on Jake and Vishal's sales floor?

A) Improper vetting of the employees meant one of them was a criminal hacker who installed the software on the network which resulted in the attack
B) An employee was able to access a poker app on his phone using the company's Wi-Fi network and may have inadvertently exposed the network to the malicious software
C) An irate customer hacked into the company's network and implanted the malicious software
D) An employee submitted his login credentials via a link in an official-looking email that appeared to be from his bosses

15) What policy would serve Jake and Vishal well going forward to secure their work network?

A) Institute a policy that states employees must never share login credentials with other employees
B) Update their antivirus software to allow for real time message filtering and malware discovery
C) Train employees and have employees sign an IT security agreement that requires them to follow specific security rules and guidelines
D) All of the above are essential for creating a secure network for the business

16) In addition to the cost and inconvenience of bringing business to a halt, and the potential
loss of proprietary company information, customer information is now potentially at risk,
putting the company in danger of enforcement action for a breach. How might Jake and
Vishal have limited their vulnerability to this enforcement?

A) They could have registered with the National Data Breach Prevention
   Association and took the 3 day training
B) They could have hired staff that were already familiar with state and federal data
   protection laws
C) They could have had a sufficient employee IT security training policy and written
   incident response procedures
D) They could have checked all inbound emails their employees had received for
   any suspicious-looking links

17) The Children's Online Privacy Protection Act (COPPA) has what distinction?

    A) It's a federal Act protecting children online, where few state laws that do so exist
    B) It allows industry to set standards that can be approved at the federal level
    C) It is always preempted by stricter state laws
    D) It can't be enforced if the data subject ages out by the time enforcement action takes place

18) GeoCities and Facebook faced enforcement action by the FTC mainly because

A) They were reckless with consumer data
B) They engaged in practices that ultimately caused financial and psychological hardship for affected consumers
C) They defied warnings from the FTC to change their business practices
D) They violated their own terms of service related to consumer privacy

19) With the new fiscal year, Cynthia chose to re-enroll in the same employer-sponsored
insurance plan as the year prior. She was relieved when a company-wide memo came out
saying that premiums would not be raised across the board this year, but was later
dismayed to discover hers would be going up by 20%. The only significant procedure she
had done at the doctor's office last year was a test to see if she was more susceptible to
possibly developing breast cancer in her lifetime. Cynthia's insurer may be in violation of
federal law because:

A) Insurance plans cannot adjust premiums based on genetic information in
absence of current illness or condition
B) Everyone else's premiums stayed flat while hers went up and no explanation was
provided
C) Insurers cannot increase premiums at any time without the State AG's approval
due to the 2014 Worker's Insurance Protection Act
D) The rise in premiums are in conflict with the collective bargaining rights in
Cynthia's employment contract

20) A Reporter from the Springfield Post has gotten tips from locals that a biopharmaceutical
firm has set up a clinical trial in town to address an outbreak of especially virulent flu. The
tips have stated trial participants are suffering severe side effects as a result of the
experimental drugs they're being given. After no one at the company returned the reporter's
calls, they sought more information about the study and its participants from the FDA under
FOIA. Why was their FOIA request denied?

    A) The HIPAA Privacy Rule states the reporter needs a valid reason to obtain the
information
    B) The Cures Act has a FOIA exemption to protect the privacy of subjects
    C) The HIPAA Security Rule mandates the reporter must fill out the proper
paperwork to submit with their FOIA request
    D) Pharmaceutical companies are exempt from most FOIA requests under a
provision in the Sarbanes-Oxley Act

21) Which of the following is not a legally valid reason for a Doctor's Office to share patient
information with a third party without the patient's consent?

    A) A radiology clinic the patient was referred to needs to know if the patient is
allergic to iodine

    B) The patient was involved in a traffic incident in the Doctor's Office parking lot and
they've received a subpoena for the camera footage

    C) The patient's insurance company needs paperwork to make the proper financial
adjustments

    D) A new physical therapy clinic private practice is opening across town and the
patient's doctor thinks the patient could be a potential client

22) A major update to HIPAA in 2009 mandated all of the following except:

A) People or businesses handling patient data on behalf of a covered entity were now required to apply the same privacy standards
B) Health Care providers who accept payment electronically were required to digitize patient records
C) The type of information provided by or collected from patients was defined and given specific privacy protections under law
D) Specific procedures to address the unauthorized loss, disclosure, or theft of patient information were implemented

23) A consumer has the right under federal law to challenge all of the following on their credit report except:

A) A default on a credit card that had a punitive APR% under laws that have since been amended to prevent such practices
B) A personal bankruptcy finalized in September 2009 appears on a credit report pulled in February 2021
C) A credit report lists a consumer's home address as an old one the consumer hasn't lived at for several years
D) A credit report shows a balance owed on a car loan that was paid off several years prior

24) The "Red Flags Rule" stipulates that

    A) Consumers with a shaky credit history are thoroughly vetted before being offered lines of credit or mortgages
    B) Consumers that engage in multiple overseas financial transactions are reported to the SEC for heightened scrutiny of such transactions
    C) Financial institutions and creditors must respond to international hacking incidents within a prescribed time frame
    D) Financial institutions and creditors must enact rules to help guard against identity theft

25) Enforcement of the Gramm-Leach Bliley Act is carried out by the following financial
regulators:

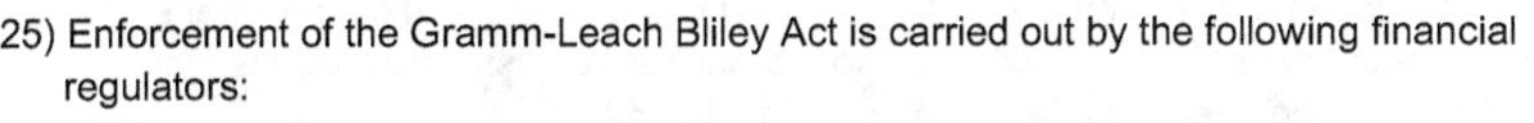

A) The FDIC, HITECH, SEC, and Federal Fiduciary Committee
B) The Federal Reserve, Office of the Comptroller of the Currency, FDIC, and SEC
C) The SEC, Federal Banking Oversight Commission, FDIC, and Dept. of Treasury
D) The FDIC, Office of the Comptroller of the Currency, Finance and Commerce
Commission, and Federal Banking Authority

26) Tammy turned 18 immediately after graduating high school and decided to attend college close to home and continue living with her parents for at least her first year. One day her father confronted her about her grades, noting she was in danger of failing chemistry, and offering to hire a tutor. Tammy was outraged and immediately called the registrar's office to complain about releasing her academic info without her permission. What was their explanation for the release of Tammy's grades to her father?

A) They explained that her father presented a Parental Rights Waiver that was recently passed into law by the state legislature

B) They explain that Tammy attends a school that only receives a small fraction of their funding from the federal government and is therefore legally considered a private institution and not subject to FERPA

C) Her father presented evidence that Tammy is considered a dependent in the household for tax purposes

D) Her father is a longtime personal friend of the dean

27) Jake and Vishal finally got past the IT security deficiencies that had plagued the launch of
their telemarketing sales business and it was thriving. Until one day, when they got a sternly
worded letter from an attorney representing an irate customer and threatening legal action
for one of their associates violating the law regarding a call the customer received on March
5th. Which of the following would not be a legal basis for the validity of the letter?

A) The customer received the call at 9:27pm their local time
B) The customer had registered on the federal Do Not Call list as of January 21st
C) The customer answered and heard only dead air for 10 seconds before hanging
up
D) The customer's caller ID could not identify the phone number or name of the
business when they received the call

28) Curtis came home from work to notice his roommate, Frank, filling out an online survey about TV watching preferences. Curtis warned Frank that he was likely having all his information tracked and would now be receiving a barrage of advertising and spam emails based on his responses. Frank told him not to worry, the law states if that were the case, there would have been a privacy policy on the website stating that his information was being collected. What state do they live in?

    A) California
    B) Vermont
    C) Delaware
    D) Nevada

29) Dina is very security-conscious and while shopping for a new cellular provider is worried about having her call logs and other similar information kept private. What Federal agency has regulations protecting this information?

    A) FTC
    B) FCC
    C) FDIC
    D) Federal Telecom Oversight Commission

30) Financial institutions are required to file a report with the Dept. of Treasury on each of the following types of transactions except:

A) When the institution suspects criminal activity associated with the transaction regardless of dollar amount
B) When the transaction is carried out by someone who is a government employee and may have a conflict of interest
C) When the transaction amount is over $5000 and is carried out by someone with known ties to international money laundering
D) When the transaction is suspicious and totals over $25,000 regardless of who carried it out

31) Which is true about businesses' ability to share information about cyberattacks they've endured from foreign hackers?

A) They are legally required to share the info under the Cybersecurity Intelligence Sovereignty Act
B) Shared information is subject to FOIA and state disclosure laws
C) They can share information with the federal government and also receive information from the federal government about hacking incidents involving other businesses
D) Businesses are encouraged to share the information with the federal government but not state and local government, as they do not have jurisdiction over federal cybersecurity laws

32) The passage of the Patriot Act greatly complicated privacy rights in the post 9/11 age. In the intervening years, restrictions have now been enacted regarding which of the federal government's data collection practices?

A) The ability to bulk collect communications involving US citizens
B) The ability to wiretap conversations involving US citizens and foreign nationals
C) The ability to collect PHI for national security matters
D) The ability to compel national security-related data from Internet Service Providers

33) When a company receives a National Security Letter, they have the option to:

A) Reject the Letter if it does not offer a specific rationale for the information sought
B) Disclose the contents of the letter to whomever would need to help supply the requested information, and to legal counsel
C) Disclose the contents of the Letter to their board of directors for guidance, even when someone on the board is the subject of the Letter's request
D) None of the above. Companies must immediately comply with all requests in a National Security Letter without divulging any of the information in the Letter to anyone but the specific addressee, pursuant to Section 702 of FISA

34) Which of the following practices are most conducive to being able to comply with e-
discovery requests?

A) Having a separate dedicated department to handle these requests
B) Having robust data retention policies
C) Having a dedicated e-discovery officer in your privacy dept.
D) Loosening data access standards so that more employees can compile data in
order to comply with requests

35) The main federal law governing workplace privacy in the US is:

A) The NRLB Workers' Bill of Rights
B) There is no overarching federal US privacy law
C) The ADA
D) ERISA

36) Employers may obtain an applicant's credit report prior to offering employment. Limits to the information they may collect are regulated by:

A) FTC and GLBA
B) NRLB and CFPB
C) FTC and CFPB
D) CFPB and DOL

37) Government agencies offer the most robust worker protections by means of:

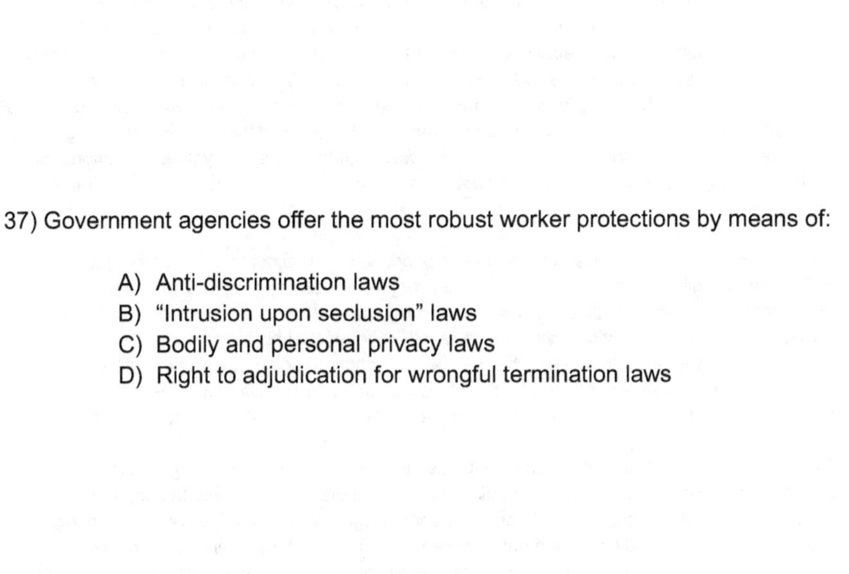

A) Anti-discrimination laws
B) "Intrusion upon seclusion" laws
C) Bodily and personal privacy laws
D) Right to adjudication for wrongful termination laws

Please answer the following 3 questions based on the following scenario:

Miguel applied at a large tech firm after seeing a recruiting advertisement on a job board site. He was offered an interview and during the interview he was asked the standard questions about his work experience, education, specific skills that he might apply to the job, and his salary expectations. As the interview went on and was seemingly going well, the conversation loosened and he was casually asked some questions about his background and nationality. When he mentioned he was a newlywed he was asked whether he and his wife planned to have children, and even felt comfortable enough to mention the difficulty they might have doing so because of a medical condition his wife has. He was a bit taken aback by these questions, but he felt as though they were asking them because he had developed a good rapport with the interviewers.

About a week later, Miguel was offered the position, which he accepted. Onboarding and training went well, and about a month into his new job he was enjoying it. One day he was called into his manager's office. His manager brought up the fact that certain employees were badmouthing the company on social media and then requested his login credentials for a social media site so that he could see whether Miguel had made any disparaging remarks about the company as well. Miguel explained he had done no such thing himself, but when pressed to then offer his login info to prove these claims, he demurred and said he would think about it.

Disturbed, Miguel immediately went back to his desk and emailed an employment lawyer he knew, from his personal email account. It was Miguel's personal laptop, as the company employed a BYOD policy. A week later, his manager again demanded his social media login credentials, and handed him a printout of the email he had sent to the employment lawyer. Miguel was stunned, and immediately offered his resignation. Miguel was asked to return his security badge, and during his exit interview was asked to sign the company's security policy, the timing of which he found odd. About a week later, a former coworker forwarded Miguel an email his former manager had sent to everyone at the company, stating Miguel had been fired for gross insubordination and repeated violation of company policy. Miguel immediately called the lawyer he had reached out to before.

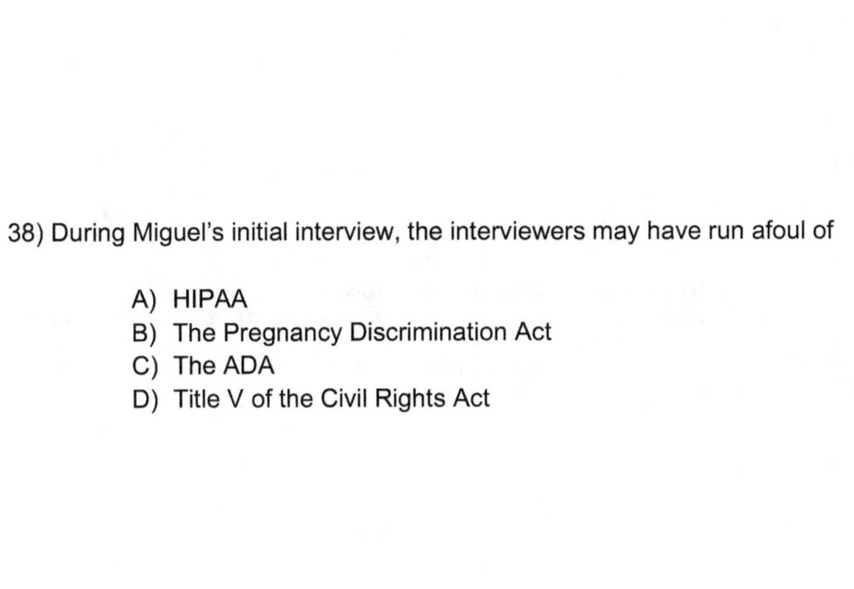

38) During Miguel's initial interview, the interviewers may have run afoul of

A) HIPAA
B) The Pregnancy Discrimination Act
C) The ADA
D) Title V of the Civil Rights Act

39) Miguel's manager acted most improperly while:

A) Requiring him to use his personal laptop for work
B) Bringing up other employees' behavior as a means of pressuring him to divulge personal information
C) Violating coworkers' privacy by mentioning the content of their social media posts
D) Asking him for his social media login credentials

40) Miguel may have grounds to sue his former employee for:

A) Defamation
B) Wrongful termination
C) Gross invasion of privacy
D) Workplace discrimination based on his race

41) The CCPA has raised important issues regarding preemption and adopting a standard
national privacy law going forward mainly because:

    A) Federal laws are vague and poorly written, and CCPA makes for a good template
for a federal framework as it already exists
    B) With increasing political polarization, certain states are becoming less likely to
follow California's lead on any legislation
    C) State laws are inconsistent and varied, while CCPA, having the most robust and
comprehensive individual privacy protections among state laws, could act as a
national template
    D) Industry that doesn't do business in California may feel left out of the legislative
process

42) Privacy concerns when it comes to marketing are most clearly manifested by:

A) Companies employing social engineering to invasively market to individuals who might otherwise make more responsible buying decisions
B) Companies utilizing aggressive subliminal or subconscious marketing strategies that lead consumers to engage in commerce without their conscious knowledge or consent
C) Companies utilizing existing business relationships to rope consumers into lengthy contracts that might otherwise inhibit them from getting better deals on the open market
D) Companies collecting and utilizing consumers' personal data and aggressively marketing to them by means of unwanted and/or excessive direct communication

43) The federal government's rule to safeguard consumer's financial data is divided into levels of security that include:

A) Administrative Security, Technical Security, Logistical Security
B) Logistical Security, Administrative Security, Cyber Security
C) Technical Security, Physical Security, International Security
D) Physical Security, Technical Security, Administrative Security

44) Which state recently instituted robust data security laws regarding financial transactions?

A) New Jersey
B) New York
C) Connecticut
D) Delaware

45) Increasingly, personal data is being collected in myriad ways from consumers just going about their daily lives. This "Internet of Things" (IOT) has caught the attention of privacy advocates, and is most pervasive:

A) In public places like subway stations and airports, where increased surveillance is capturing more data than people realize
B) At doctor's offices and hospitals, where things like vital signs and medication histories are captured by intake and medical devices and shared with various entities
C) In personal spaces like people's homes or cars, where appliances, cell phones, and smart speakers are constantly collecting data in order to provide advanced functionality
D) In retail sales environments, like grocery stores or large chain "big box" stores, where buying habits linked to credit cards and even browsing habits captured by surveillance under the guise of security are being used for marketing purposes

ANSWER KEY

1) B	24) D
2) A	25) B
3) C	26) C
4) D	27) D
5) B	28) A
6) B	29) B
7) C	30) B
8) A	31) C
9) C	32) A
10) D	33) B
11) C	34) B
12) B	35) B
13) A	36) C
14) D	37) A
15) D	38) B
16) C	39) D
17) B	40) A
18) D	41) C
19) A	42) D
20) B	43) D
21) D	44) B
22) C	45) C
23) A	

1) The correct answer is **B) Proposed legislation being debated in the US House of Representatives.** As your business operates across the US, it may be important to know about local and state laws, in addition to individual cases before the Supreme Court that may create precedent, but federal legislation is the most relevant to staying on top of current and emerging privacy laws and regs. This question is an example of how you must choose the best answer, even though more than one may be technically correct. You will encounter many questions like this on the exam.

2) The correct answer is **A) Consumers received direct advertisements from an affiliated company after agreeing online they had the option, and then declining to opt in to receive such advertisements.** This is an example of an entity violating their own privacy policy – a big no-no with the FTC. While B) is somewhat feasible, it's not as good an answer as A), C) is not relevant, and D) is a throwaway answer.

3) The correct answer is **C) The specific types of information covered by the law and who enforces potential violations.** These are the basics of understanding how a new law affects a business's privacy practices. Whom does it affect and what are the repercussions of not following it? A) is not relevant and while B) and D) may be good things to know, they are not essential to understanding how the new law will affect you and your business.

4) The correct answer is **D) Common Law.** This is a tricky question, of which you will see many on the exam. An established pattern over time is known as Common Law, while Case Law is an element that builds Common Law. The other two choices are not applicable to the question.

5) The correct answer is **B) A judgement ordering him to move the fence at his own expense or an equivalent amount owed to Mr. Jones to accomplish this.** You are likely to encounter some questions like this on the exam, wherein a scenario is presented that doesn't have much or anything to do with privacy law, in order to test your handle on the subject matter while taking you out of the privacy paradigm. A) is an example of a criminal penalty, whereas this is obviously a civil dispute. C) is incorrect as it is highly unlikely the two neighbors entered into a contractual agreement that calls for arbitration when they became neighbors, and D) is a bit extreme for a fenceline dispute.

6) The correct answer is **B) Agreeing to stop the negligent actions and pay a fine, without officially admitting wrongdoing.** This question and answer represent a very convoluted way of testing your knowledge of what a Consent Decree is. This is something you will encounter frequently on the exam. It works to make it very difficult to master the subject matter with just rote memorization of terms and definitions. Instead, it will present scenarios that test your mastery of

the subject matter beyond what you can absorb via simple flash cards. A) would effectively do the opposite of what she is being asked to do by her boss, and C) and D) are fantasy.

7) The correct answer is **C) Do a full inventory of all the data in your possession and organize it according to sensitivity, figure out the flows of data within your organization, and create an accountability plan for safeguarding it.** A) is something you can do, but it may not be especially helpful, and is certainly not a comprehensive approach. B) isn't particularly helpful, and D) is not possible to do without cataloging what data you are working with and how to classify it.

8) The correct answer is **A) Protection from liability after a breach according to many state laws.** While B) is hypothetically a good reason, it's clearly not as good an answer. C) is a throwaway answer and D) is simply incorrect.

9) The correct answer is **C) Create a Privacy Notice displayed on the company website and posted in public places.** A) is not realistic, B) is insufficient, and D) is incorrect.

10) The correct answer is **D) All of the above are examples of when individuals must be asked to "opt-in" to sharing their personal information.** All presented choices are elements of privacy rules from different laws from varying industries.

11) The correct answer is **C) Inform the individual of ways they could improve their credit regardless of their credit score or results of the background check.** Employers are under no obligation to play credit counselor. They are legally required to do A) and B).

12) The correct answer is **B) Fair Information Practice organizations that develop specific guidelines or principles that address consumer access and redress.** FIPs and FIPPs are terms you will encounter frequently in studying for the exam. A) does not exist, and C) and D) are basically aspirational ideas.

13) The correct answer is **A) Do background research on the vendor and have them sign a contract with the same privacy standard language as exists within the company's primary privacy policies.** B) and C) are fine ideas, but they are not systematic methods for reducing risk. D) is fantasy.

14) The correct answer is **D) An employee submitted his login credentials via a link in an official-looking email that appeared to be from his bosses.** Many people struggle with the

long scenario questions on the exam. They are often filled with misdirection, irrelevant information, and fluff, designed to confuse you. It is important to read and if necessary, re-read them carefully. The correct answer to this question is an example of either Phishing or Spear Phishing, which are the most common vectors for ransomware infection. A) and C) while arguably hypothetically possible, are unlikely, and B) is infeasible.

15) The correct answer is **D) All of the above are essential for creating a secure network for the business.** All options presented are basic tenets of IT security.

16) The correct answer is **C) They could have had a sufficient employee IT security training policy and written incident response procedures.** This is an example of "CYA," wherein a company is shielded from breach incident liability if they can document employees were properly trained and procedures were in place to mitigate risk. A) is a made-up entity, and B) and D) are highly unrealistic options.

17) The correct answer is **B) It allows industry to set standards that can be approved at the federal level.** COPPA is an example of a Co-Regulatory Model. All the other answers are incorrect.

18) The correct answer is **D) They violated their own terms of service related to consumer privacy.** A potentially tricky question, as there are arguably several correct answers, with D) being the best. While A) is correct, it's too vague, B) is more an element of arguing punitive damage amounts, and C) is more an example of violating an existing Consent Decree.

19) The correct answer is **A) Insurance plans cannot adjust premiums based on genetic information in absence of current illness or condition.** This is an element of GINA. B) has no relation to any federal law, C) references a hypothetical state law, and D) represents a potential union issue, which is not mentioned in the scenario.

20) The correct answer is **B) The Cures Act has a FOIA exemption to protect the privacy of subjects.** While A) is somewhat arguably correct, it is too non-specific, C) is made up, and D) is incorrect as Sarbanes-Oxley has nothing to do with the subject of the question.

21) The correct answer is **D) A new physical therapy clinic private practice is opening across town and the patient's doctor thinks the patient could be a potential client.** All the other answers are examples of when PHI can be disclosed without authorization under HIPAA.

22) The correct answer is **C) The type of information provided by or collected from patients was defined and given specific privacy protections under law.** Another potentially tricky question, all of the others refer to new rules introduced under HITECH, amending HIPAA, while C) refers to elements of HIPAA that were already in existence before HITECH became law.

23) The correct answer is **A) A default on a credit card that had a punitive APR% under laws that have since been amended to prevent such practices.** All the other answers are things a consumer can have corrected under the FCRA.

24) The correct answer is **D) Financial institutions and creditors must enact rules to help guard against identity theft.** The Red Flags Rule was created under FACTA, effectively updating the FCRA.

25) The correct answer is **B) The Federal Reserve, Office of the Comptroller of the Currency, FDIC, and SEC.** Every other answer has at least one made up agency. This is an example of a question wherein you'll need to recall minutiae. Anytime the question refers to an agency or entity that comes up repeatedly in the study material, there's a good chance you'll be drilled on specific details of it on the exam.

26) The correct answer is **C) Her father presented evidence that Tammy is considered a dependent in the household for tax purposes.** It's an obscure, strange aspect of FERPA, but it's made clear in the study materials. A) refers to a hypothetical state law, and FERPA is not preempted by state law, B) is incorrect because an institution that utilizes any federal funding is subject to FERPA, and D) is a throwaway answer.

27) The correct answer is **D) The customer's caller ID could not identify the phone number and name of the business when they received the call.** All the other options are violations of the Telemarketing Sales Rule, however if a business's name and number do not appear on a consumer's ID on one occasion, there's no way to prove it wasn't a technical issue on the consumer's end.

28) The correct answer is **A) California.** The scenario presents an example of provisions under the CCPA. When in doubt, California is always a decent guess in terms of states that have privacy protections that exceed those available via federal laws.

29) The correct answer is **B) FCC.** The FCC will most often be the oversight body when it comes to privacy laws related to communications. The FTC and FDIC are typically the bodies that oversee business and financial transactions, and D) is a made-up agency.

30) The correct answer is **B) When the transaction is carried out by someone who is a government employee and may have a conflict of interest.** All the other answers are examples that necessitate SARs under the Bank Secrecy Act.

31) The correct answer is **C) They can share information with the federal government and also receive information from the federal government about hacking incidents involving other businesses.** A) is a made-up Act, B) is incorrect and D) is not relevant.

32) The correct answer is **A) The ability to bulk collect communications involving US citizens.** As a result of the Edward Snowden revelations, the USA FREEDOM Act of 2015 curtailed the government's ability to bulk collect data. All the other answers are examples that are still permissible under the USA PATRIOT Act.

33) The correct answer is **B) Disclose the contents of the letter to whomever would need to help supply the requested information, and to legal counsel.** A) and C) would be running afoul of the law and D) is incorrect and not relevant to the question.

34) The correct answer is **B) Having robust data retention policies.** That answer is a succinct summation of the Sedona Conference. A) and C) are potentially good ideas, but don't get to the core issue, and D) is incorrect.

35) The correct answer is **B) There is no overarching federal US privacy law.** A) is made up. One could make an argument that C) is correct, however the study material makes it clear that federal law governing workplace privacy is lacking. D) is not a good answer relative to the topic.

36) The correct answer is **C) FTC and CFPB.** Those are the agencies that regulate workers' privacy rights related to employers collecting background information of workers or potential workers, with CFPB created under the FTC. All the other answers mention an agency that is not related to the question's topic.

37) The correct answer is **A) Anti-discrimination laws.** While all the other options offer some degree of protections for worker privacy, the most comprehensive and effective are laws that prevent hiring and workplace discrimination.

38) The correct answer is **B) The Pregnancy Discrimination Act.** In inquiring about Miguel's plans for himself and his wife to have a baby, the employer may be in violation of the Act. A) is a possible answer because Miguel mentioned his wife's medical condition, but that information was volunteered. C) is incorrect as a disability was never discussed and D) is incorrect as it's Title VII and not title V of the Civil Rights Act that pertains to workplace discrimination.

39) The correct answer is **D) Asking for his social media login credentials.** A) is an increasingly common practice in workplaces and not on its face improper, B) and C), while unseemly, are not in and of themselves clear legal violations of worker privacy.

40) The correct answer is **A) Defamation.** B) is incorrect as Miguel offered his resignation, C) is unlikely as there's little expectation of privacy for workers in private industry, and D) is incorrect as there was no indication from the details in the scenario Miguel faced any discrimination based on his race or ethnicity. Employers must be very careful when talking about former employees in order to avoid possible civil action for Defamation.

41) The correct answer is **C) State laws are inconsistent and varied, while CCPA, having the most robust and comprehensive individual privacy protections among state laws, could act as a national template.** A) seems like a good answer on the surface, but C) is better. B) and D) are throwaway answers.

42) The correct answer is **D) Companies collecting and utilizing consumers' personal data and aggressively marketing to them by means of unwanted and/or excessive direct communication.** A) and C) are more issues of business ethics than violations of privacy and B) is a throwaway answer.

43) The correct answer is **D) Physical Security, Technical Security, Administrative Security.** Every other option has one made up level of security relative to the GLBA Safeguards Rule.

44) The correct answer is **B) New York.** In 2017 New York passed laws that are more stringent and detailed than similar GLBA requirements. Expect to see numerous questions on the exam that deal with specific state laws.

45) The correct answer **is C) In personal spaces like people's homes or cars, where appliances, cell phones, and smart speakers are constantly collecting data in order to provide advanced functionality.** All the other answers present examples of potential privacy vulnerability but only C) relates to IOT.

www.ingramcontent.com/pod-product-compliance
Lightning Source LLC
Chambersburg PA
CBHW060915130726
48001CB00006B/2242